"It's not a bad job, but I hate the hours."

D1566791

Andrews and McMeel

A Universal Press Syndicate Company

Kansas City

ISBN: 0-8362-1768-3
Library of Congress Catalog Card Number: 94-72370

ATTENTION: SCHOOLS AND BUSINESSES

"It makes you miss the old punch clock, doesn't it?"

"Care to make a donation to a non-profitable corporation?"

"Relax! It should be here any minute."

"Say, do we get Labor Day off?"

"Damn! I left a Kleenex in my pocket."

"Work with me, will ya? ... This is front page material!"

5

"Why yes, we do have something available next Thursday."

"I hope this doesn't catch on."

"We're looking for someone with a little less experience."

"It's an all-new environmentally enriched organic food by-product that has revolutionized lawn care!"

"Hey, look — a perfectly good manager!"

WAISGLASS/COULTHART

"Don't sell your shares yet, Harry …
pet rocks are a long-term investment."

"Still haven't figured out the electronic mail
system, huh, Bob?"

"Face it, Don. We're losers."

"Well, we worked out the details. Now,
if we can just agree on the main points …"

"No matter what I say, these farmers
won't keep their hands off me."

"Quit complaining! Times are hard,
and we've got to be versatile."

"That's it — no more free coffee!"

"I'm not sure, but I think they want us
to pee on this stuff."

"Say, I thought this was a management washroom."

"I'll trade my bologna for your tuna fish."

"We don't get much business, but we're always profitable."

"Don't worry, Jimmy. If there's fish in this lake, we'll find them."

"Take it from me, pal — you don't
have to follow the herd."

"I've got to find a job that's more politically correct."

"And you thought they didn't care."

"It's a market opportunity that also solves our chemical waste problem."

"Sure, I'd like to start my own business …
but, frankly, I think it's too risky."

"Don't worry about it, kid. This is Hell.
You don't have to go outside to smoke."

"I'm afraid we don't have the support
of the labor movement on this one."

"You see, son, this way I can spend
more time with you."

"It's more powerful than conventional sharpeners."

"Do you have anything in a pump?"

"Ms. Spencer is here for her assertiveness training."

"The kids want to know what's next on the agenda."

"I guess you're not interested in our lawn mowers either?"

"How many times do I have to tell you? … Don't draw on the walls!"

"And it gets worse … they lost my luggage too!"

"Hey, only three more months, and my student loan will be paid off!"

"My client refuses to answer on the grounds that he may incriminate me."

"We've been robbed!"

"This is my boss's idea of a raise."

"I don't see why we pay more for less calories."

16

"Last cigarette? They told me this was a taste test."

"What did you expect? You hired a turtle!"

"I just thought we could be more competitive."

"My card."

"Next time we go out looking for babes, we'll take my car."

"Then, I said, 'Why go to a big city when everything we need is right here in the pasture?' But, nooo …"

"Uh, not you, Bob … I meant other people can't take criticism."

"It's always something … mittens, boots, hats. I'm telling you, you'd lose your head if it wasn't screwed on."

"It's part of the creative process."

"Why me? I didn't do anything."

20

"Quick, somebody hire a temp!"

"What do you suppose it means?"

"Things aren't working out, Edwards. Have you considered a job with our competition?"

"I guess this ends our roundtable discussion."

"If your house burns down, we'll replace the defective unit absolutely free!"

"You know, there is a cafeteria downstairs."

"Say, we're looking for someone with your skills in our collections department."

"What makes you so damn special?"

If at first you don't succeed, embezzle.

"Trust me, kid, you don't get this kind of experience in journalism school."

"He's right, the law says we have to negotiate in good faith."

"It helps managers to read between the lines."

"Okay, we're out. Now what?"

"I'm not really awake until I have my morning coffee."

"I'm sorry, we don't do lawyers here."

"Stop complaining. It's going first class."

"I preferred the course on looting and pillaging."

"We've had a few drive-bys, but no serious offers."

"According to these tests, you've got rigor mortis."

"I'm sure it won't be a problem … you fellas look like a good risk to me."

"It seems you have a problem with authority figures."

"Paper or plastic bags?"

"We try to save something for the environment."

"Then it's agreed … there's no room for further cuts in production."

"When were you declared surplus?"

"How much more to fly nonstop?"

"My brother works on an ant farm that's unionized ... and they don't settle for crumbs."

"No one's punishing you, Greenham. Just think of this as a marketing opportunity."

"Always listen to the customer, Millwood. But don't take no for an answer."

"George, it appears you misunderstood me when I asked you to organize this department."

"I know this scam ... once you cut it, I have to keep coming back."

"We couldn't find any good candidates for this position, so we're going to promote you instead."

"C'mon in, Harvey. I'm sure we can settle this nasty little grievance."

"I suggest you start small ... you can always upgrade later."

"If you learned from your mistakes, Carl, you'd be a genius."

"Will somebody turn down the damn air conditioner?!"

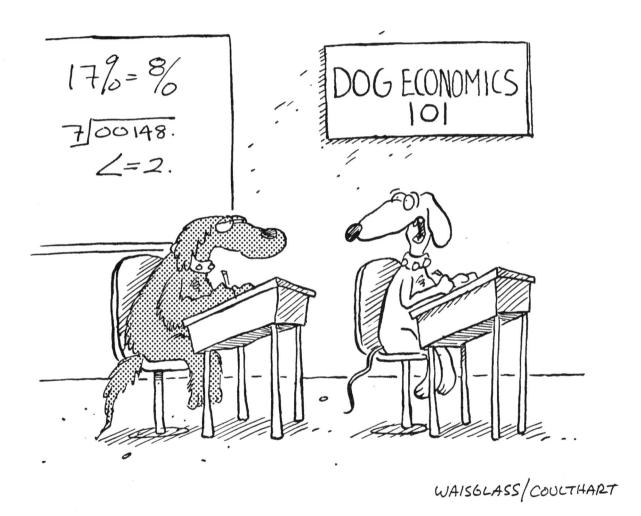

"Remember when all we had to do was fetch?"

"Kid, there are two types of people in this world … those who generalize, and those who don't."

"Some people here think you're taking advantage of our family benefits."

"You mean you didn't know this was a seasonal job?"

"Try to think of this as a government job."

"… and I won this for winning
so many awards!"

"No, Felix, you have to act natural
or the magazine won't buy it."

"I don't think it's a good idea we go into business together."

"I can put him in a sandwich, but I have to charge you more."

"It says here, there's a greater chance of being struck by lightning than winning the lottery."

"It's decaf, and no one could tell the difference."

"Your horse refuses to come out until he talks to a union representative."

"I trusted him more when he had a whip."

"It seems to me, Flemming, you have the skills we want on our management team."

"I'm okay ... see? Nothing's broken!"

"You know, some of the guys in the flock
think you're showing off again."

"And this just in: The fire downtown
is spreading to other buildings."

"A funny thing, Dalton ... your request for a
transfer suddenly came through."

"Yeah, yeah, the check is in the mail."

"It's a worker exchange program. The old guy
is grazing in the back 40."

"You sheep just don't know when to trust your lawyer."

"Give me three large bass … and don't bother to wrap them."

"In the local news … employees at Buxley's Dry Cleaners are still out on strike."

"I had to pull a few strings, but this time the agency promises to send a real knock out!"

"There's no sex discrimination here because we fired all the men."

"We need to know your next of kin."

"Hey look, Spriggs ... this moron left the keys in the car!"

"And when did you join Smokers Anonymous?"

"I'm not sure … what does it
look like to you?"

"Scotty, here, says you're three weeks
behind on his allowance."

"For a lesser fine, I can turn in three other
speeders and a litterbug."

40

"… now let's see how you react to scenes of your employees leaving early."

"No need to thank me — I needed the practice."

"I'm not blaming you, Lewis. I'm delegating responsibility."

"I've repaired it 38 times, and I still can't figure out why it breaks every morning."

"Faulkner, here, got a government grant to study the effects of UV rays."

"I need fire insurance, quick!"

"I need another $50."

"You gave away 60 billion toys and didn't get one receipt?!"

"You can't plead insanity."

"I thought *you* had the keys."

"All I have left are videos of my kids at the beach."

"They've joined the free-range chicken movement."

"Your 10:00 marketing meeting was rained out."

"Has it been six months already?"

"Maybe you should just wake up earlier."

"I hate junk mail."

"You can't divorce your wife on the grounds that she refuses to laugh at your jokes."

"Whose stupid idea was it to take over a tar company."

"I guess it wasn't a good idea to scale down just before Christmas."

"Gesundheit."

"I don't have any emotional problems ... can I borrow yours?"

"Quick, somebody call a lawyer!"

"I hate these employee motivation seminars."

48

"I don't think reverse psychology is going to work."

"Management thinks I can offer a new perspective."

"I think I finally found a no-smoking program that works."

"I don't see your dog around, Mr. Morriscey. Guess I really put a scare into him yesterday."

"Nowadays, you can't make ends meet by just farming."

"It looks much worse when you see the big picture."

"That's *Dr.* Idiot to you!"

"It must have been a power surge."

"Carlos here is our foreign sales agent.
... At least, I think he is. I can't understand
a word he says."

"Well, at least you got over
your fear of heights."

"I will not resign. I will not resign.
I will not ..."

"OK, Eddie, you can go home now."

"I quit. You guys give me the willies."

"Do not light barbecue before reading page 6."

"We've had a few complaints, Finlay, that you're not a team player."

"At Hogwell Industries, every employee is entitled to three weeks' vacation."

"It says, 'Best before November 17'."

WAISGLASS/COULTHART

"I got the idea this morning in the shower."

"I told you not to drink so much."

"There's nothing worse than bad imitation crab."

"Sure I have a last request ... fire my lawyer!"

"Great idea! Why didn't anyone think of this before?"

"See, I told you we wouldn't be safe from insurance salesmen."

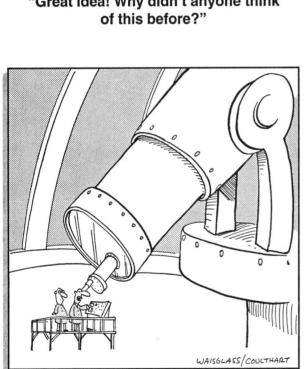

"There ... just between the Big Dipper and the Pepsi ad."

"Gentlemen, I suggest we stop promoting managers on the basis of seniority."

"I thought this was a health club."

"Yes, it is a nasty paper cut, but you don't qualify for handicapped parking."

"I quit my last job because everyone there hated my guts."

"... and this is our corporate planning group."

"We've got too many bureaucrats!
Submit a requisition for more people
to study the problem."

"Do you have anything for twisted, mean-
spirited, overbearing supervisors."

"It's wedged in there pretty tight, Mr. Mayor.
But it's not as bad as last time."

"It seems you misunderstood when I said
you should visualize the audience naked."

"I wouldn't worry about a few lousy opinion polls!"

"Wow — 38 days without a cigarette."

"And on Tuesdays they go to ASPCA meetings."

"I'm sorry, Earl, but that's all the budget allows for our witness protection program."

"Vegetarians give me gas."

How Vincent van Gogh really lost his ear.

"We want employees who will give 100% of themselves."

"So, Byron, tell us how the product testing is going."

"No, Fifi ... the mouse. Get the mouse!"

"Hey, wait a minute ... only a man would wear **green pumps with a blue chiffon dress!**"

"I don't want to mention any names, but one of us is on a diet!"

"My interior decorator is also a taxidermist."

"What's to know?! Give 'em a lullaby, some formula, and before you know it — you've got a footprint on the bottom line."

"It's clearly a conflict of interest. I strongly suggest you don't accept any more milk and cookies."

"Okay, but don't tell anyone … you know how rumors get started."

"I don't think our employees should be training these robots."

"It doesn't look good … the health and safety committee doesn't meet until next Friday."

"No need to worry, Ms. Harris. We fixed the leak."

"I just invented the power company. Here's my bill."

"And for the last five years, I worked at the Windmore Fan Company."

"I hate Christmas. All this smiling makes my face hurt."

"Okay, fellas, I have a counter-offer ..."

"And this slightly used paper clip is a small token of our appreciation."

"Watch what you say — this room may be bugged."

"It's only until the postage meter is repaired."

"Oh, you want the gun shop on the second floor — this is the toy department."

"It works like a scarecrow, but it keeps managers away."

"At first, I thought this computer dating service was a bit of a scam ..."

"You obviously misunderstood. In any case, how long were you able to keep it to the grindstone?"

"I'm not sure — maybe this *is* his analysis of the West Coast market."

"Our video monitoring system lets you get rid of annoying door-to-door salespeople."

"Yes, sir, I believe we have our costs under control."

"You're not getting my lunch money this time."

"… then he asked if I was ready to climb the corporate ladder."

"Don't worry … that little weasel doesn't have the guts to fire anyone!"

"Our extended warranty covers everything except parts and labor."

"Where did you say you got your communications degree?"

"We're looking for a celebrity endorsement."

"It has time-released painkillers, so you'll never have another headache."

"I think it's great that you can work at home."

"I guess we did give you the wrong suitcase — and, boy, is our face red."

"I think it's time to review our corporate strategy."

"Just two more gallons and we get a free set of steak knives."

"Why do people who work sitting down make more money than those standing up."

"When I said we missed the deadline ... he came unglued."

"My dad is a lecherer at the university."

"After 25 years, this stuff still cracks me up."

"It's very pretty, but I was hoping you would take my ideas more seriously."

"Honey, where do we keep the elbow grease?"

"Well, all right ... if you think it's art."

"OK, dig here ... I think we found another quarter."

"No excuses. It's overdue … now, hand over the coconuts!"

"Of course, this high-performance computer has only one crucial flaw …"

"Well, you did say you wanted an office with a view."

"We value underlings like you, Grimsby, because they know their place."

"Sorry, Brimswell, you've been traded to
Accounting for three calculators and
a fax machine."

"You know, with some lemon and a few
peppers, we could be quite delicious."

"It's for a good cause."

"Thanks to Finstead, here —
Christmas will now be on June 8th."

"We want to improve our image."

"This office floor plan was favored by 96% of the laboratory rats tested."

"Geez, I had no idea there was a Nobel Prize for accounting."

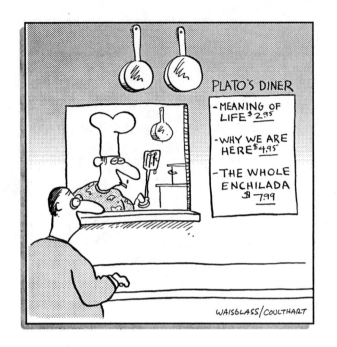

"This should make it more sporting."

"Good news ... I've negotiated a settlement that should cover your legal fees."

"I didn't see nothin'. Did you?"

"No matter how cold it is outside, never go into a liquor store wearing a ski mask."

"And don't chat with the customers —
it scares them."

"I hope Lou's Liquor Store gets hit again.
Last night's ratings sky-rocked."

"And the first party of the first part,
herein known as Cathy ..."

"He forgot to pay the bill."

"But you're gonna miss 'Seinfeld' tonight."

"Our interest rates are very reasonable ... wouldn't you rather take out a loan?"

"In other words, *smile* while you're being screwed."

"I'm telling you, Grimsby, technology is changing the way we work."

"I can assure you, we've never had a complaint."

"Wow! Cool earrings, Dad."

"One extra large guy, no onions."

"Congratulations, Mr. Rouse, you're a free agent!"

"I've tried everything to get it to work — but now it just keeps saying *union, union, union!*"

"Is it me, or does the day seem to drag on forever?"

"And for your personal comfort and safety, we recommend you do not eat our in-flight meal."

"You misspelled *graduate*."

"I don't think it heard you ... say it louder."

Just before lunch, Marvin learns about the process of natural selection.

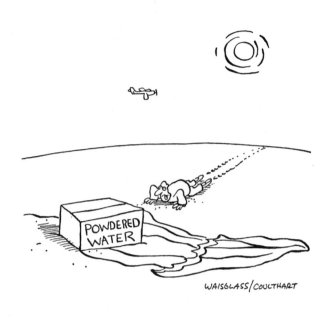

"I empowered my employees, and got laid-off for being redundant."

"I need a leave of absence."

"Wow — another episode of
'Three's Company'!"

"So, you went to Harvard and learned to
delegate authority, then what happened?"

"It must be one of those infomercials."

"Your account must be overdrawn."

"I can communicate anywhere in the world — but I have nothing to say."

"Let me assure you, sir, I will personally seek out the calculator responsible for those errors."

"I'm not here to rescue you, Mr. Harris — I'm your wife's attorney."

"My chiropractor says I should find a branch that's more ergonomically correct."

"If there was an embezzler here, I'd know about it."

"Get out there and improve morale
or you're fired!"

"Sure, we're over managed, but we can't
afford to make mistakes."

"Your doorbell must be broken."

"It says, 'For a good time, call Cleo'."

"Stop this sacred cow stuff before you convert the entire herd."

"Maybe you didn't notice, kid, but we have a dress code here."

"Geez, do they always turn white like that?!"

"… Well, OK, but I need three pieces of identification."

"I'd rather have the raise."

"We've been told to balance the budget."

"Let me get this straight — it's a last-minute sell-off and no singles allowed."

"Let's not panic — this may be just a coincidence."

"She doesn't really work here, but it's one hell of a deterrent."

"We must be on a mailing list."

"It's people like you who give this business a bad name!"

"How did a cute little tax deduction turn into a major liability?"

"This isn't the drug-testing program I had in mind."

WAISGLASS/COULTHART